Early TRANSPORTATION Encyclopedias

TRAINS

by Priyanka Lamichhane

Early Encyclopedias

An Imprint of Abdo Reference
abdobooks.com

abdobooks.com

Published by Abdo Reference, a division of ABDO, PO Box 398166, Minneapolis, Minnesota 55439.
Copyright © 2024 by Abdo Consulting Group, Inc. International copyrights reserved in all countries.
No part of this book may be reproduced in any form without written permission from the
publisher. Early Encyclopedias™ is a trademark and logo of Abdo Reference.
Printed in China
102023
012024

THIS BOOK CONTAINS
RECYCLED MATERIALS

Editor: Carrie Hasler
Series Designer: Candice Keimig

Library of Congress Control Number: 2023939669

Publisher's Cataloging-in-Publication Data

Names: Lamichhane, Priyanka, author.
Title: Trains / by Priyanka Lamichhane
Description: Minneapolis, Minnesota : Abdo Reference, 2024 | Series: Early transportation
    encyclopedias | Includes online resources and index.
Identifiers: ISBN 9781098292959 (lib. bdg.) | ISBN 9798384910893 (ebook)
Subjects: LCSH: Railroad trains--Juvenile literature. | Locomotives--Juvenile literature. | Railroads--
    Juvenile literature. | Railroads--History--Juvenile literature. | Vehicles--Juvenile literature. |
    Transporation--Juvenile literature. | Encyclopedias and dictionaries--Juvenile literature.
Classification: DDC 629.224--dc23

CONTENTS

All Aboard!

Trains have been around for more than 200 years. They are used all over the world to carry people and goods.

Trains changed the way people live and work. The first railroads were built in England in the 1600s. They were called wagonways. They were wooden tracks used for horse-drawn wagons.

In the 1800s, iron was placed on a wooden wagonway. This made it stronger. A steam locomotive was added. Together, they created the first railroad!

Today, there are all sorts of trains. Some travel long distances. Others take short trips. There are trains that go under the ocean. Some trains even go through mountains!

How Trains Work

All trains move on tracks that have two parallel rails. The train wheels fit on the tracks. The tracks guide the wheels. Early trains were powered with steam. Today, some trains run on diesel. It is used to create electricity that moves the train. Other trains run on electricity that comes from outside the train. Maglev trains use electricity and magnets. Together, they pull a train forward.

FUN FACT!

Extra steam comes out of the steam dome. The train whistles when the steam is released.

How a Steam Train Works

The first step in powering a steam train is burning coal to boil water. This makes steam. The steam goes through tubes. It builds pressure. The pressure pushes the pistons. The pistons push the wheels. The train moves!

steam dome

smokestack

firebox

boiler tubes

piston

TIMELINE

1804: The first steam-powered locomotive was built.

1830: The first steam-powered passenger railroad opened in England.

1869: The first cross-country railroad was built in the United States.

1883: The Orient Express made its first run.

1900s: Steam trains were replaced with trains that run on diesel fuel.

1964: Japan's high-speed bullet train was built.

1990s: The Channel Tunnel was built, linking the United Kingdom and France.

2000s: Shanghai Maglev—the high-speed, magnet-powered train—began running.

2016: The world's highest railway opened in Tibet.

2023: Japan is developing the Alfa-X. It will be the fastest train in the world.

B&O No. 51

The B&O No. 51 did not run on steam. It was one of the first diesel locomotives in the world. This made the train easier to take care of. It ran faster than steam engines too.

FUN FACT!

The No. 51 had a nose shaped like a bulldog's.

Year Built:
1937

Type of Engine:
Diesel

How Fast It Moved:
30 mph (48.3 kmh)

How Long It Ran:
16 years

This train ran on the Baltimore & Ohio Railroad. The train was painted blue and gray.

In 1953, the No. 51 stopped running. It is now on display at the B&O Railroad Museum.

Best Friend of Charleston

The Best Friend of Charleston was a steam locomotive. It was the first to carry passengers in the United States on a regular schedule.

FUN FACT!
The Best Friend's train tracks were made of metal and wood.

Year Built:
1830

How Fast It Moved:
25 mph (40.2 kmh)

Type of Engine:
Steam

How Long It Ran:
6 months

Best Friend of Charleston 1830

USA 22

The Best Friend changed travel in the area. Before the railroad was built, travel depended on the weather. People traveled by foot or by horse. Roads got dusty in the heat. They were muddy after rain. It was also slow to travel by boat.

Did You Know?

The train's first trip was 6 miles (9.7 km) long. It started in Charleston, South Carolina.

Flying Scotsman

The Flying Scotsman is a steam locomotive. It has been carrying passengers for more than 100 years!

When the Flying Scotsman was built, it had the most powerful engine of any kind. It was the first train in the United Kingdom to reach 100 miles per hour (160.9 kmh).

Year Built:
1923

Type of Engine:
Steam

How Fast It Moves:
100 mph (160.9 kmh)

FUN FACT!

Today, the Flying Scotsman is still used for special tours and events.

In 1963, the train stopped running every day. By this time, it had traveled 2 million miles (3.2 million km). That's the same distance as 80 trips around the world!

Locomotion No. 1

The Locomotion No. 1 picked up coal from mines in England. Then it pulled the coal to a seaport.

FUN FACT!

Visitors can see a copy of the Locomotion No. 1 at the Head of Steam museum in England.

Year Built:
1825

Type of Engine:
Steam

How Fast It Moved:
15 mph (24.1 kmh)

How Long It Ran:
16 years

Did You Know?

Steam trains had two people in charge: the fireman and the engineer. The fireman built the fire and kept it burning. This kept the water boiling. The water turned into steam, which powered the train. The engineer watched the train's speed. He also made sure all of the machines on board were working.

This steam locomotive ran on the Stockton and Darlington Railway. When the railway opened, many people came to see the Locomotion.

The Locomotion No. 1 didn't have any brakes! But the coal cars did. The brakes on the train cars helped stop the train.

Mallard

Most steam trains during the 1930s went no more than 100 miles per hour (161 kmh). But, in 1938, the Mallard broke the speed record of any steam train by going 126 miles per hour (202.8 kmh). The previous record was 114 miles per hour (183.5 kmh). The Mallard is still the fastest-ever steam train.

The Mallard was built to be smooth and strong on the outside. This helped it go fast. Under the train, a little pipe released sand. The sand helped the wheels stick to the tracks. The locomotive also had an early speed recorder. It was under the fireman's seat.

FUN FACT!

The Mallard is named after the mallard duck.

Year Built:
1938

Type of Engine:
Steam

How Fast It Moved:
126 mph
(202.8 kmh)

How Long It Ran:
25 years

Pioneer Zephyr

The Pioneer Zephyr was the first diesel-powered locomotive made of all stainless steel. Before this, they were made with iron. Iron is a very heavy metal. Stainless steel is lighter. The lighter metal meant the Zephyr could move faster.

Year Built:
1934

Type of Engine:
Diesel

How Fast It Moved:
110 mph (177 kmh)

How Long It Ran:
26 years

FUN FACT!

The first train car pulled by the Zephyr also had a post office.

1st regular service trip of the **ZEPHYR** Lincoln, Omaha, Council Bluffs, St. Joseph and Kansas City Nov. 11, 1934

1st streamline train in America to be established in daily operation

BLISS R BOWMAN, SOUTH ST. JOSEPH, MO.

The Zephyr pulled only three train cars. The first had the engine. The second carried luggage and people. It also offered food for passengers. The third carried only passengers.

Did You Know?

The Pioneer Zephyr's nickname was the "Silver Streak."

Puffing Billy

The Puffing Billy has been running in Melbourne, Australia, for more than 100 years. It was first built for people who lived away from larger towns. The train made it easier for them to travel.

Year Built:
1900

How Fast It Moves:
16 mph (25.7 kmh)

Type of Engine:
Steam

The Puffing Billy takes passengers on a two-hour ride. Part of the ride is through a forest. The cars on this train have open sides. People can sit facing out. They can enjoy the sights.

FUN FACT!

The Puffing Billy still runs on its original track.

Royal Hudson

The Royal Hudson ran on the Canadian Pacific Railway. It traveled long distances.

This locomotive had a water heater pump. The pump would heat water before it was sent to the boiler. Since the water was preheated, the boiler needed less energy to make steam.

This train also had a system to place coals in the fire. No fireman was needed.

Year Built:
1937

Type of Engine:
Steam

How Fast It Moved:
More than 100 mph
(160.9 kmh)

How Long It Ran:
60 years

Did You Know?

In 1939, the king and queen of England rode this train across Canada. The king liked his ride so much that he added *Royal* to the train's name. Before that, it was just called the Hudson.

Spirit of Altoona 1361

The Spirit of Altoona 1361 was a steam locomotive that ran on the Pennsylvania Railroad. During the 1910s and 1920s, the Pennsylvania Railroad built many locomotives and trains in a large shop in Altoona. The Spirit of Altoona was one of the most famous trains built there.

This train had an engine called the K4 Pacific. It was powerful and lasted a long time. There were 350 locomotives built with these engines. They carried passengers between Pittsburgh and New York. Later, the Pennsylvania Railroad grew. Trains traveled to more cities.

Year Built:
1918

How Fast It Moved:
87 mph (140 kmh)

Type of Engine:
Steam

How Long It Ran:
35 years

Stephenson's Rocket

People in England wanted more trains to travel between cities. There was a competition. Which locomotive was the best? Which one could do the job? It was Stephenson's Rocket.

Year Built:
1829

Type of Engine:
Steam

How Fast It Moved:
Up to 30 mph (48.3 kmh)

How Long It Ran:
10 years

La ROCKET a inauguré la section Liverpool-Manchester 1830

ព្រះរាជាណាចក្រកម្ពុជា ២០០ៜ
រូបសណ្ឋិយ

ROYAUME DU CAMBODGE
POSTES 1995
200ᴿ

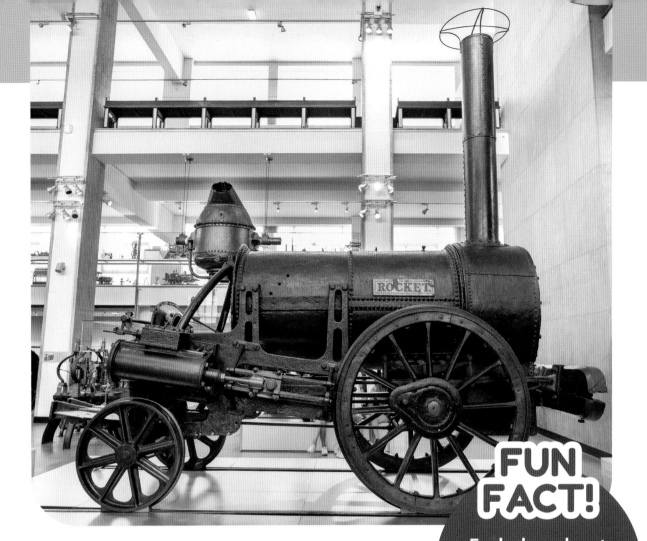

The Rocket pulled trains on the Liverpool & Manchester Railway in England. They were the first trains in the world to carry passengers from city to city.

Trains pulled by the Rocket also carried goods. Before then, goods were moved on boats. But boats were slow. The Rocket moved items a lot faster.

Tom Thumb

The Tom Thumb was a small steam locomotive. It ran on the Baltimore & Ohio Railroad. This locomotive was a bit different. It had no roof.

Year Built:
1830

Type of Engine:
Steam

How Fast It Moved:
10 to 14 mph (16.1 to 22.5 kmh)

How Long It Ran:
About 1 year

FUN FACT!
The Tom Thumb became famous. Its image was put on a postage stamp in 1952.

Tom Thumb 1829

200f

REPUBLIQUE DE GUINEE
OFFICE DE LA POSTES GUINEENNE
OPG 1996

PETER COOPER'S TOM THUMB 1829-30 BALTIMORE & OHIO R.R.

The Tom Thumb was the first fully working American steam locomotive. Before it came along, horses were used to pull carriages on the B&O Railroad. This locomotive changed transportation. Steam-powered trains began replacing horses and carriages.

Trevithick Steam Carriage

The Trevithick Steam Carriage was the first vehicle for passengers that was powered by steam. It took its first trip around London, England, in 1803. There were about eight passengers on board.

Year Built:
1801

Type of Engine:
Steam

How Fast It Moved:
4 to 9 mph
(6.4 to 14.5 kmh)

How Long It Ran:
About 1 year

FUN FACT!

The Trevithick Steam Carriage led the way for more steam-powered vehicles, including trains.

This was the first vehicle that could power itself. But it was destroyed when its engine caught on fire.

Richard Trevithick, its inventor, built another steam carriage. But he did not have enough money to build anymore after that.

Union Pacific Big Boy

The Union Pacific Big Boy was the world's largest steam engine. It was 132 feet (40.2 m) long. It weighed more than 1 million pounds (453,592.4 kg).

Year Built:
1941

Type of Engine:
Steam

How Fast It Moved:
80 mph
(128.7 kmh)

How Long It Ran:
20 years

The engine needed to be big and strong. It carried heavy freight long distances. Special sets of wheels helped it pull such weighty cars.

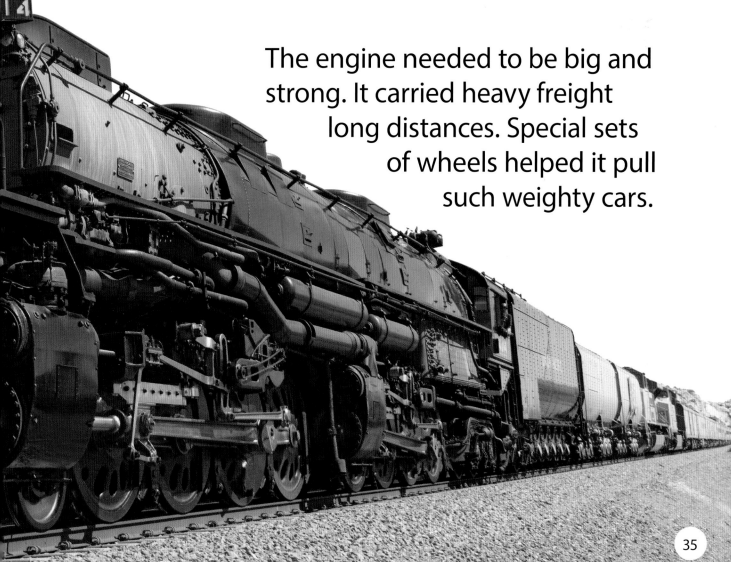

Belmond Andean Explorer

The Belmond Andean Explorer moves through parts of Peru. It is a luxury train. This means it is fancy. It has areas for passengers to eat and sleep. It even has a restaurant.

FUN FACT!

Passengers can listen to live music on board this train.

Year Built:
2017

Type of Engine:
Diesel

How Fast It Moves:
35 mph
(56.3 kmh)

This train travels on high railroads. Passengers can see the Andes Mountains. They can also see Lake Titicaca. It is in the mountains. It is one of the highest lakes in the world.

Did You Know?

Lake Titicaca is located between Peru and Bolivia. The lake has floating islands. The islands were made by the people from the area. They made the islands out of reeds.

Belmond Royal Scotsman

The Belmond Royal Scotsman takes passengers through Scotland. It travels through an area called the Highlands. This area has lots of peaks and valleys. On the ride, passengers can see castles and lakes.

Year Built:
1985

Type of Engine:
Diesel

How Fast It Moves:
60 mph
(96.6 kmh)

FUN FACT!
When the Royal Scotsman is ready to leave, a Scottish piper starts to play music.

There is a special car at the end of the Royal Scotsman. It has big windows and a balcony. It is where people go to get a good view of things outside.

Blue Train

The Blue Train travels across South Africa. The trip is about 990 miles (1,593.3 km) long.

Year Built:
1946

Type of Engine:
Diesel

How Fast It Moves:
56 mph
(90.1 kmh)

FUN FACT!

The Blue Train was named after its cars, which are painted blue.

There is a large car full of big windows at the back of the train. It is the best place to watch the scenery. Passengers can look at the mountains. They can see wildlife too! There is a library on board this train. The restaurant car can fit 42 people.

Did You Know?
The trip across South Africa on the Blue Train takes 27 hours.

Ghan

The Ghan is the longest passenger train in the world. It travels north and south across Australia's Outback. It is a long trip! The Outback is the center of the country. It is a huge desert region.

Year Built:
1929

Type of Engine:
Diesel

How Fast It Moves:
85 mph
(136.8 kmh)

Did You Know?

The Ghan train is named after camel drivers from the country of Afghanistan. They came to work in the Outback more than 120 years ago.

The Ghan travels 1,851 miles (2,978.9 km). The first time this long trip was taken was about 20 years ago. Before then, the railroad was not long enough. The train could not go as far.

Maharajas's Express

The Maharajas's Express travels to different parts of India. It is like a palace inside. In fact, the carriages look like ones that Indian royalty once rode in.

The Maharajas's Express has 23 carriages in all. Passengers can stay in 14 of the carriages. The largest one is like an apartment! It has two bedrooms and a bathroom. There is even a living room and a dining room.

Year Built:
2010

Type of Engine:
Diesel

FUN FACT!

Each carriage on the Maharajas's Express is named after a gemstone such as a diamond or pearl.

Orient Express

The Orient Express has been around for more than 100 years. The original train ran across Europe. It had routes from London, England, all the way to Istanbul, Turkey.

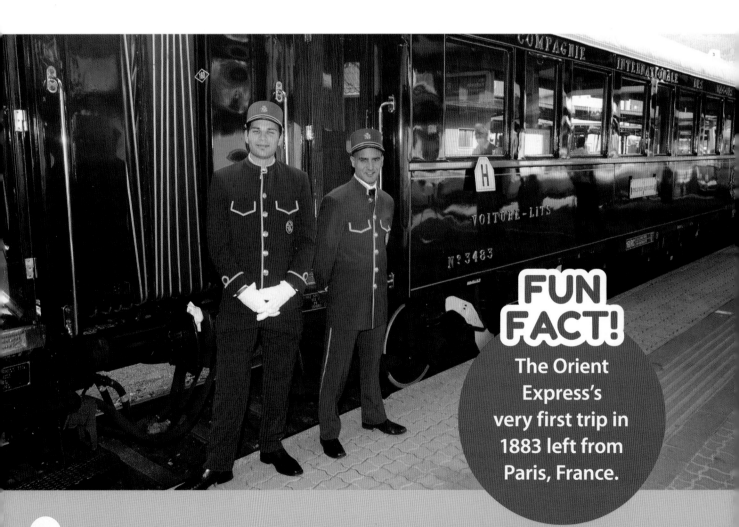

FUN FACT!

The Orient Express's very first trip in 1883 left from Paris, France.

The original train no longer runs. But newer models of it do. These trains use restored carriages that are almost 100 years old. The Orient Express still travels to many places around Europe.

Year Built:
1883

Type of Engine:
Diesel

How Fast It Moves:
99.4 mph
(160 kmh)

Palace on Wheels

The Palace on Wheels takes people all around north India. The trip takes 8 days. There are restaurants on board. The bedrooms have lots of decorations. There is even a place where passengers can exercise.

FUN FACT!

The Palace on Wheels is India's oldest fancy train.

The train cars are painted on the outside. They are covered with shapes and patterns. There are 41 train cars on this train. The train can carry 82 passengers.

Year Built:
1982

Type of Engine:
Diesel

Did You Know?

Many years ago, Indian royalty traveled on trains like this one. The cars from some of these older trains were reused to make the Palace on Wheels.

Rocky Mountaineer

At first, the Rocky Mountaineer ran only in Canada. It took passengers through the Canadian Rocky Mountains. Now it travels through the Rocky Mountains in both Canada and the United States.

It has a special train car that is covered in windows. Passengers can see views of mountains, rivers, and rainforests.

FUN FACT!

This train only runs during the day. Why? So passengers can always see all the sights!

Year Built:
1990

Type of Engine:
Diesel

How Fast It Moves:
105 mph
(169 kmh)

Did You Know?
The Rocky Mountaineer runs on what used to be called the Canadian Pacific Railway. It is now called CPCK. The railway was started in 1881.

Rovos Rail

The Rovos Rail runs in parts of Africa. It takes passengers on short and long trips. Some last two days. Others last two weeks.

The train made its first trip in 1989. Back then, the train ran only in South Africa. It only had seven train cars. Now the train is longer and travels to more places.

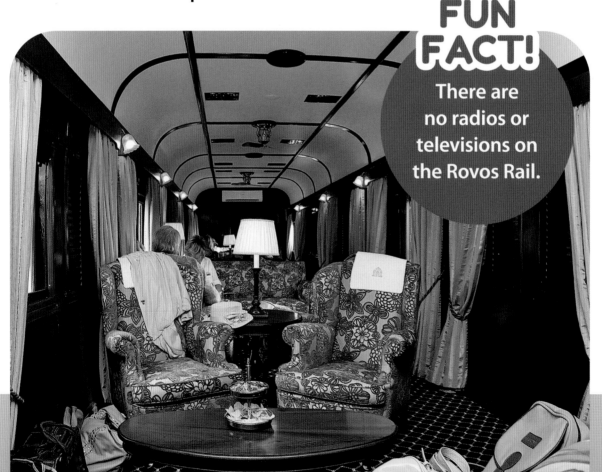

FUN FACT!

There are no radios or televisions on the Rovos Rail.

Year Built:
1989

Type of Engine:
Diesel or electric

How Fast It Moves:
37 mph
(59.5 kmh)

Did You Know?

All of the Rovos Rail trains were old steam-powered locomotives at one time. The trains were made to look new again. Today, they run on diesel or electric power.

Seven Stars in Kyushu

This train takes passengers around the Japanese island of Kyushu. There are seven regions in Kyushu. That is how the Seven Stars train got its name!

Year Built:
2013

Type of Engine:
Diesel

How Fast It Moves:
62 mph (99.8 kmh)

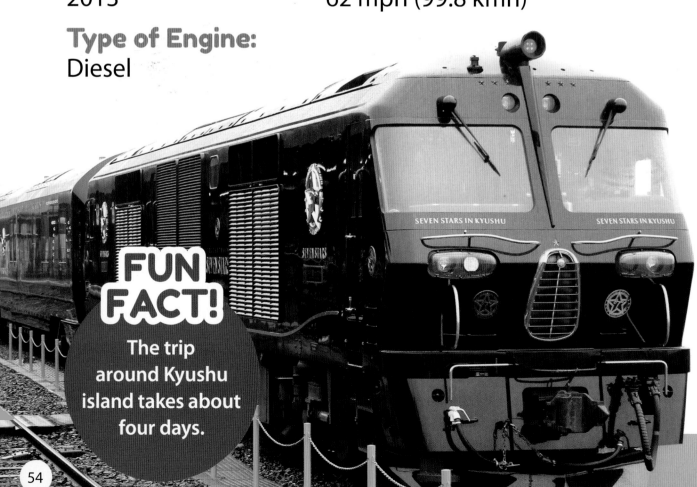

FUN FACT!
The trip around Kyushu island takes about four days.

This train can carry 28 passengers. There are seven cars. Passengers can sleep in five of the cars. There is also a restaurant car. There are large windows. Passengers can enjoy all the sights along the trip.

Al Boraq

The Al Boraq is a high-speed train in Morocco. The train runs between the cities of Casablanca and Tangier. This journey takes just over two hours. Before this high-speed train began service, the trip took more than four hours.

Year Built:
2015

Type of Engine:
Electric

How Fast It Moves:
199 mph
(320.3 kmh)

The Al Boraq has eight passenger cars and two levels. The train runs on electricity. There is a large car that serves food.

Amtrak Acela

The Amtrak Acela trains are the only high-speed trains in the United States. There are 20 of them.

One train travels between Washington, DC, and Boston, Massachusetts. There are 13 stops along the way. A lot of people live in these areas. They want a fast way to travel.

Acela trains have six cars. The train cars do not come apart like other train cars do. This helps keep the ride smooth.

Year Built:
2000

Type of Engine:
Electric

How Fast It Moves:
150 mph
(241.4 kmh)

AVE S-103

The AVE S-103 is Spain's high-speed train. It can carry more than 400 passengers.

The train car where the driver sits has a glass wall in the front. Passengers can see what the driver sees.

The AVE S-103 goes from the city of Madrid to the city of Barcelona in only two and a half hours. This trip is 405 miles (651.8 km) long.

The AVE S-103 is able to tilt. It can lean as it goes around a curve. This helps the train go fast.

Year Built:
2007

Type of Engine:
Electric

How Fast It Moves:
217 mph (349.2 kmh)

FUN FACT!

The Sagrada Familia cathedral is located in Barcelona, one of the stops of the AVE S-103.

CR400 Fuxing

The CR400 Fuxing train is part of a network of high-speed trains in China. They can go more than 200 miles per hour (321.9 kmh). These trains are built for speed. They are made of a light metal. This helps them go fast.

FUN FACT!

High-speed trains are also known as bullet trains.

There are two types of CR400 trains. One has eight train cars. Another has 16 cars. More than 1,200 people can ride the 16-car train!

Year Built:
2017

Type of Engine:
Electric

How Fast It Moves:
217 mph (349.2 kmh)

ICE3

The ICE3 is Germany's fastest train. It is also one of the fastest high-speed trains in Europe.

Year Built:
2000

Type of Engine:
Electric

How Fast It Moves:
205 mph
(329.9 kmh)

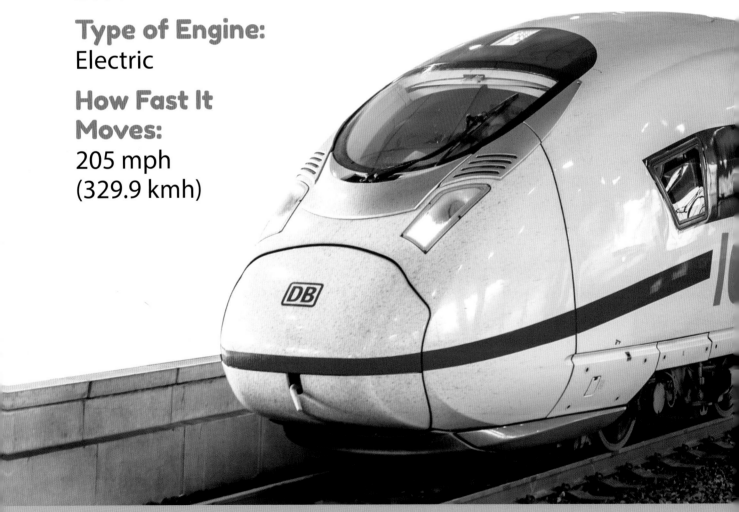

The ICE3 has a restaurant on board. It also has a quiet car and an area just for kids.

Some of the ICE3 trains travel outside of Germany. They go to places such as France and the Netherlands.

FUN FACT!

There is a type of ICE train called the ICE T. It can tilt to go around curves.

HIGH-SPEED TRAINS

JR East E5

The JR East E5 is Japan's high-speed train. It can carry more than 730 passengers.

Year Built:
2011

Type of Engine:
Electric

How Fast It Moves:
200 mph
(321.9 kmh)

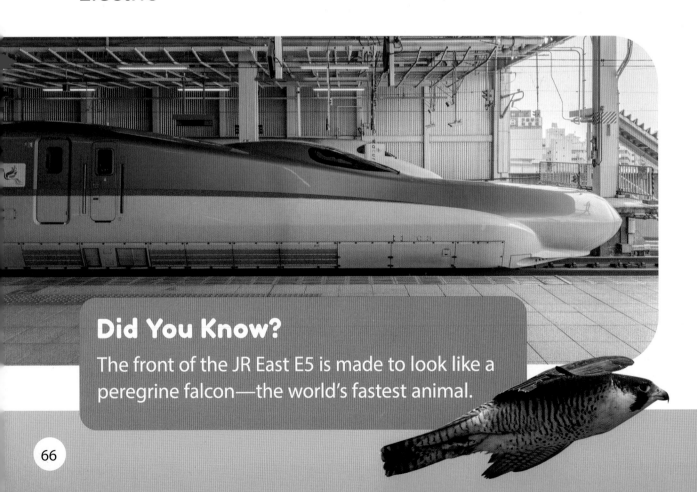

Did You Know?

The front of the JR East E5 is made to look like a peregrine falcon—the world's fastest animal.

When some trains go into a narrow tunnel, the air pressure inside the tunnel can increase suddenly. This can cause a loud noise called tunnel boom. But the JR East E5 has a long nose. It is 50 feet (15.2 m) long! The train's nose helps to prevent tunnel boom.

This modern train has a suspension that keeps it stable at high speeds. Another system allows the train to tilt around curves.

KTX Train

KTX stands for "Korea Train Express." The KTX is a long train. It has 18 train cars! It can fit more than 900 people.

The KTX takes riders all over South Korea. The first route for the KTX was from the capital city of Seoul to Busan, the country's second-largest city.

FUN FACT!

More than 100,000 people ride the KTX each day.

Year Built:
2004

Type of Engine:
Electric

How Fast It Moves:
190 mph
(305.8 kmh)

Did You Know?
The first train in Korea began running in 1899. It went only 12 miles per hour (19.3 kmh).

Shanghai Maglev

The Shanghai Maglev is the fastest train in the world. It travels from one of China's airports to a train station in Shanghai. The total distance is 19 miles (30.6 km). The trip takes only seven minutes!

Did You Know?

China has the world's largest high-speed train system.

Year Built:
2004

Type of Power:
Electromagnets

How Fast It Moves:
286 mph (460.3 kmh)

What is special about this train? It does not need a track or wheels! Maglev trains run using magnets. The trains sit slightly off the ground. Magnets pull the trains forward. Since the Shanghai Maglev train does not touch the ground, it is a very smooth ride.

FUN FACT!

Passengers can play tennis on the Shanghai Maglev, even when it is moving!

TGV

The TGV is France's high-speed train. The train service started in 1981 with just one line. It went from Paris to Lyon. From there, the number of train routes grew.

Year Built:
1981

Type of Engine:
Electric

How Fast It Moves:
199 mph
(320.3 kmh)

FUN FACT!

TGV stands for *Train à Grande Vitesse*, which means "high-speed train" in French.

In 2007, the TGV train broke a speed record. It went 361 miles per hour (581 kmh). There were some people on board at the time. When the train got to top speed, some of the riders did not feel well.

Did You Know?

The TGV serves four train stations in Paris. The busiest is the Gare du Nord. More people pass through this train station than anywhere else in Europe.

Chongqing Rail Transit

The Chongqing Rail Transit is an intracity rail system. That means it runs within the city. It also connects to villages just outside the city. It is located in Chongqing, China.

FUN FACT!

The Chongqing Rail Transit is a monorail train. This means the train runs on one rail.

Year Built:
2005

Type of Engine:
Electric

How Fast It Moves:
47 mph (75.6 kmh)

More than 17 million people live in Chongqing. The train was built so there would be fewer cars on the road. Cars make a lot of pollution. They create traffic.

Delhi Metro

The Delhi Metro is one of the most used metros in the world. Trains have between six and eight cars. Two of the cars are used for power. The rest are for passengers.

Year Built:
2002

Type of Engine:
Electric

How Fast It Moves:
56 mph
(90.1 kmh)

One train on the Delhi Metro can carry more than 1,000 passengers. About 5 million people ride the Delhi Metro every day.

Hong Kong MTR

Hong Kong's MTR train system has 10 train lines. There are 98 stations along these lines.

Hong Kong is made up of islands. Some of the trains go from one island to another. The trains travel through tunnels. The tunnels run underwater.

Did You Know?

Double-deck railroad bridges help make room for all the trains.

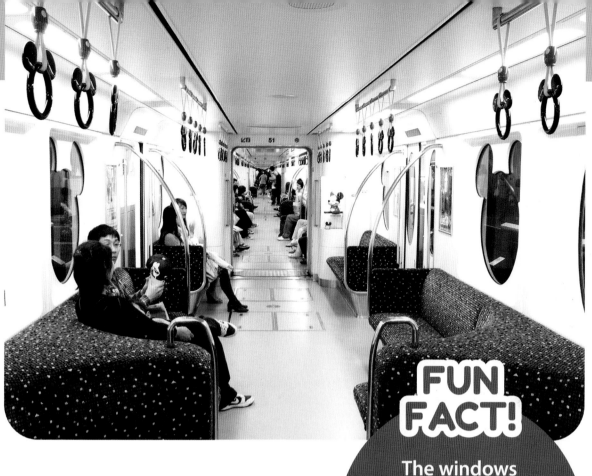

FUN FACT!

The windows and the handholds on the train to Hong Kong Disneyland are shaped like Mickey Mouse!

Hong Kong is home to a Disneyland resort. There is an MTR train line that takes people to it. These trains run on their own. They don't have a driver!

Year Built:
1979

Type of Engine:
Electric

How Fast It Moves:
84 mph (135.2 kmh)

InterCity 125

The InterCity 125 ran in the United Kingdom for more than 40 years. The train traveled very quickly through many cities. The cars were specially made to keep sound out. This meant it was a quiet ride.

Year Built:
1976

How Fast It Moved:
125 mph (201.2 kmh)

Type of Engine:
Electric or diesel

How Long It Ran:
41 years

Over the years, newer train models were built. These new trains are called the Hitachi Class 800. They go 140 miles per hour (225.3 kmh). That's a lot faster than the original InterCity 125 trains.

FUN FACT!

The Hitachi Class 800 train was made in Japan.

Lisbon Tramway

The Lisbon Tramway is a group of trams. The trams travel around Lisbon, Portugal. The first electric tram started running in 1901.

Year Built:
1901

Type of Engine:
Electric

How Fast It Moves:
43 mph
(69.2 kmh)

The number 28 tram is the most popular. It goes through the oldest parts of the city. Most of the trams are yellow. Some are red.

Lisbon has 58 trams. Most are like the number 28. They are old streetcars from a long time ago.

London Underground

The London Underground is also called the London Tube. It was built in 1863. It is the world's first underground railroad.

FUN FACT!

Some train cars on the London Tube have curved doors.

Year Built:
1863

Type of Engine:
Electric

How Fast It Moves:
60 mph (96.6 kmh)

Before the late 1800s, people used steam trains. The steam trains made the air dirty. By 1890, the trains were electric. This helped keep the air clean.

Today, the London Underground has 272 train stations and 11 train lines. The trains are red, blue, and white. There are different types of trains that run on the railway system.

New York City Subway

The New York City Subway has been around for a long time. It started running in 1904. Back then, lots of people were moving to the city. The subway was a way to help people get around.

Year Built:
1904

How Fast It Moves:
55 mph (88.5 kmh)

Type of Engine:
Electric

Today, the train cars are all silver. There are 10 cars on each train. There are special tracks for express trains only. Express trains only make one or two stops. They go extra fast!

Réseau Express Régional

The Réseau Express Régional (RER) train system runs in and around the city of Paris, France.

Year Built:
1969

Type of Engine:
Electric

How Fast It Moves:
86 mph
(138.4 kmh)

FUN FACT!

The Eiffel Tower is only a six-minute walk from one of the RER's train stations.

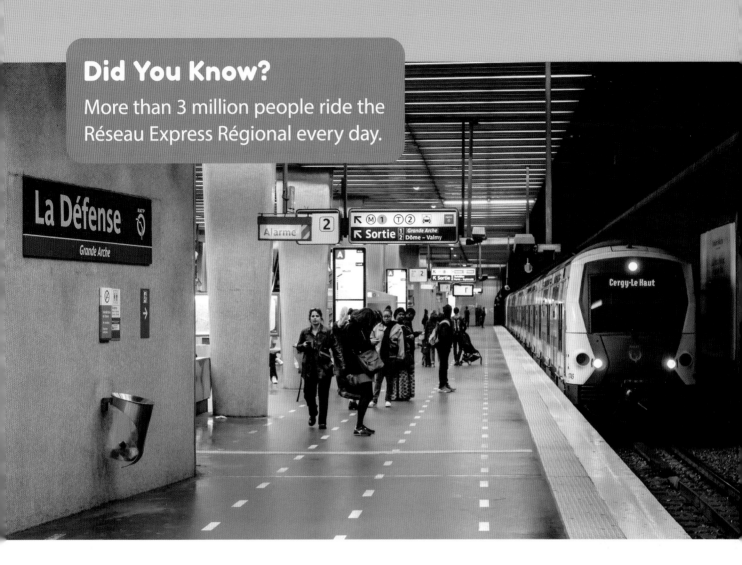

The system has five train lines and 246 stations. Each line uses a different kind of train. Some are commuter trains. Some connect to the airport. One connects to Disneyland Paris.

The system also has express trains. These trains do not make many stops. This means passengers get from one place to another much faster.

San Francisco Cable Cars

The San Francisco Cable Cars were built to help people move up the city's steep hills. The cable cars are pulled with cables. These cables are underground.

Each car has a bell. It is used to tell people there is a cable car coming. Some people use the cable cars to get to work. Others hop on to tour the city.

FUN FACT!

At one time, there were more than 600 cable cars running. Today, there are only 45 running.

Year Built:
1873

Type of Engine:
Electric

How Fast It Moves:
9.5 mph (15.3 kmh)

Did You Know?

The San Francisco Cable Car system is the last cable car system in the world that is not automatic. This means a person has to move a lever to make the cars move.

Sound Transit

Sound Transit is the train system for the city of Seattle, Washington. The system has five train lines with 39 stations. The trains have two to three cars each.

Sound Transit also has a commuter train. It is called the Sounder. It takes passengers to towns outside the city. It runs on two lines and makes 12 stops. It has two levels. Each train car can fit 148 people.

Year Built:
2000

Type of Engine:
Electric or diesel (Sounder)

How Fast It Moves:
55 mph (88.5 kmh);
79 mph (127.1 kmh)
(Sounder)

Sunrise Izumo

The Sunrise Izumo is a train that runs in Japan. It goes from Tokyo to Izumo and back. It makes different stops along the way.

Year Built:
1998

How Fast It Moves:
81 mph (130.4 kmh)

Type of Engine:
Electric

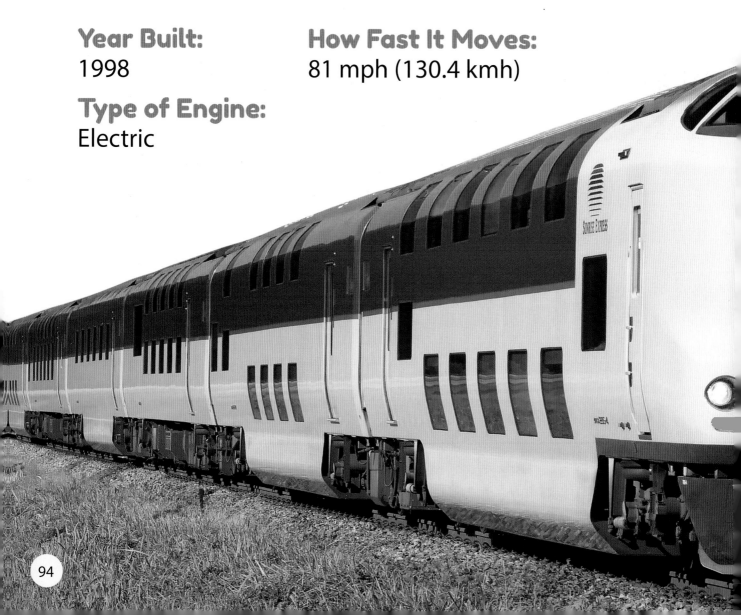

SUNRISE EXPRESS

The Sunrise Izumo is a sleeper train. It has two levels. There are small bedrooms on each level. Some sleep one person. These rooms have large windows to enjoy the sights. Other bedrooms sleep two. Passengers can also order food on the train.

Amtrak Auto Train

The Amtrak Auto Train is a passenger train. But it also carries vehicles! It travels from an area near Washington, DC, to Florida.

Year Built:
1983

Type of Engine:
Diesel

How Fast It Moves:
70 mph
(112.7 kmh)

FUN FACT!

The Auto Train can carry vehicles, which are loaded into the back.

The Amtrak Auto Train is the only train in the country that takes vehicles along for the ride. It can carry 650 passengers and 330 vehicles. The vehicles are driven across ramps and into freight cars.

Beijing-Lhasa Z21

The Beijing-Lhasa Z21 travels to Tibet. Tibet is in the Himalayas. These are the tallest mountains in the world. The train tracks are as high as 16,640 feet (5,071.9 m) above sea level. The weather is cold. The ground that holds the tracks is almost always frozen.

FUN FACT!

The Beijing-Lhasa Z21 can carry 900 passengers.

The air is very thin so high up. This can make passengers feel sick. Why? Because there is not as much oxygen to breathe. Extra air is pumped into the train cars. This helps passengers feel better!

Year Built:
2006

Type of Engine:
Diesel

How Fast It Moves:
75 mph
(120.7 kmh)

California Zephyr

The California Zephyr runs from Chicago, Illinois, to San Francisco, California. Along the way, the train goes through the Rocky Mountains. One of the train cars has windows from top to bottom. It is called the observation car. From this car, passengers can see the sights.

Year Built:
1983

How Fast It Moves:
79 mph (127.1 kmh)

Type of Engine:
Diesel

There are lots of tunnels along the way. Why? Tunnels are short-cuts through the mountains. The California Zephyr goes through the Moffat Tunnel. It is the highest point of any Amtrak railroad. It is 9,200 feet (2,804.2 m) above sea level.

Comboios de Portugal

The Comboios de Portugal travels all over Portugal. Portugal is a small country in Europe. It does not take long to get across it from north to south or from east to west.

There are three different types of trains that run on the railway. One train type runs in a city and just outside of it. The second type stays within the country. The third travels to the country next door—Spain. The Alfa Pendular is the fastest train on this railway. It takes people around Portugal.

Year Built:
1999

Type of Engine:
Electric

How Fast It Moves:
155 mph
(249.4 kmh)

FUN FACT!
The first railway line in Portugal was built in 1856.

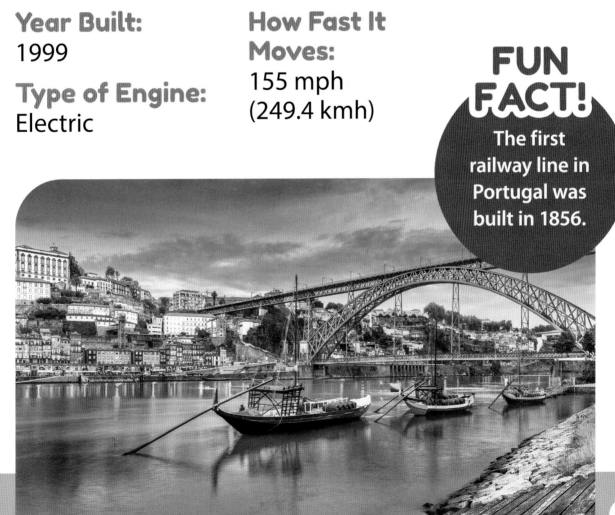

Eurostar

The Eurostar is a popular train service in Europe. It takes people from the United Kingdom to France, Belgium, and the Netherlands.

Year Built:
1994

Type of Engine:
Electric

How Fast It Moves:
198 mph
(318.7 kmh)

FUN FACT!

The Eurostar can carry 900 passengers.

Eurostar trains are high-speed trains. This means they move fast. Each train has 16 train cars. One of the most popular routes goes underwater! The train goes through the Channel Tunnel. Cars can go through the tunnel too.

Glacier Express

The Glacier Express travels through the Swiss Alps. The Alps are a mountain range in Switzerland. The Glacier Express is slow for a train. It is built for sightseeing.

Year Built:
1930

How Fast It Moves:
24 mph (38.6 kmh)

Type of Engine:
Electric

FUN FACT!

The train has huge windows, so everything outside is easy to see.

The train travels through lots of tunnels. It goes over many bridges. There is one that is very tall. The bridge is called the Landwasser Viaduct. It is 213 feet (64.9 m) high.

Did You Know?

The Glacier Express travels over 291 bridges and 91 tunnels on its route.

360° Machu Picchu Train

The 360° train runs in Peru on the Inca Rail. It goes to an old site called Machu Picchu. The train runs through a tropical forest. It also goes through the mountains. The ride to Machu Picchu takes less than two hours.

Year Built:
2009

Type of Engine:
Diesel

The 360° got its name because passengers can see all around them in a circle, which has 360 degrees! Each train has huge windows to see the sights. There are even windows on the ceiling.

Trans-Siberian Railway

The Trans-Siberian Railway is the longest passenger railway in the world. It goes across Russia.

There are different types of trains that travel on the railroad. One is the Golden Eagle Trans-Siberian Express. Traveling on the train is like staying in a moving hotel. Some cars have rooms where riders can sleep. There is also a restaurant and a living room.

Year Built:
1916

How Fast It Moves:
186 mph (299.3 kmh)

Type of Engine:
Steam

Did You Know?

All Trans-Siberian trains have a restaurant wagon where travelers can enjoy Russian dishes.

Autorack Trains

Autoracks are train cars that carry vehicles. These trains move more vehicles around the United States than any other type of freight transportation.

Year Introduced:
1920s

Type of Engine:
Diesel

How Fast It Moves:
70 mph
(112.7 kmh)

FUN FACT!
Some autoracks are enclosed. The cars ride inside the train.

Each autorack has two levels. Why? So they can fit more cars and pickups inside. The vehicles drive up a ramp and into the autorack. Their wheels are locked into place with a strap. Then large doors at the back of the autorack are closed and locked.

Autorack trains, like all freight trains, have a speed limit of 70 miles per hour (112.7 kmh). This allows these heavy trains to travel safely and save fuel.

Boxcar Trains

A boxcar looks just like its name says: a box! Boxcar trains carry everything from canned food to drinks to paper. Boxcars can be up to 60 feet (18.3 m) long.

Year Introduced:
1830s

How Fast It Moves:
70 mph (112.7 kmh)

Type of Engine:
Diesel

There are different kinds of boxcars. And there are different kinds of doors. Some doors slide shut. There is also a kind of door called a plug. A plug door slides and plugs into place, sealing up the boxcar. All doors on a boxcar are located in the middle.

FUN FACT!

The very first boxcars were made of wood. Today, they are made of steel.

Coil Car Trains

Coil car trains carry coiled steel. Coiled steel is a metal sheet that has been rolled up.

   The train cars that move the coils are made just for this job. They have spaces that can fit different sizes of coils. The steel fits perfectly in the spaces. The coils don't move around.

Year Introduced:
1960s

Type of Engine:
Diesel

How Fast It Moves:
70 mph (112.7 kmh)

Flatcar Trains

Flatcars were the first type of railcar. They are long and flat. They have no walls and no roof.

Flatcars carry big and heavy things. They also carry things that are wide or tall. The materials on a flatcar are tied down tight.

Some flatcars carry large pipes, beams, and machines. Others carry shipping containers or farm equipment such as tractors. Some are used to carry parts of railroads such as tracks. They take them to places where a railroad needs to be fixed.

Year Introduced:
1820s

How Fast It Moves:
70 mph (112.7 kmh)

Type of Engine:
Diesel

Hopper Trains

Hopper train cars are used to carry wheat, sugar, sand, and other loose items. A hopper train car opens from the top. There is a door on the roof called a hatch.

Year Introduced:
1830s

How Fast It Moves:
70 mph (112.7 kmh)

Type of Engine:
Diesel

A substance is poured in through the open hatch. When the hatch is closed, it is sealed tight. It doesn't let anything get in.

There is a chute at the bottom of the hopper. When the chute is opened, the loose material slides out into a container.

FUN FACT!

Some hopper cars are brown. When they form a train, they are called worm trains!

Refrigerated Car Trains

Refrigerated train cars are used to move food that can spoil if it gets too hot. They carry fruits, vegetables, meats, and fish. They carry dairy products too.

Year Introduced:
1877

How Fast It Moves:
70 mph (112.7 kmh)

Type of Engine:
Diesel

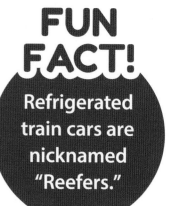

FUN FACT!
Refrigerated train cars are nicknamed "Reefers."

Most refrigerated train cars are painted white. Lighter colors reflect heat. It takes less energy to keep the cars cool. Air inside the cars flows to every corner. This way, the temperature stays the same for all the food. The doors of the cars have a tight seal. This keeps the cold air in and the hot air out!

Tanker Trains

Tanker trains safely move liquids from one place to another. They carry them in tanks. The tanks are large cylinders.

Year Introduced:
1865

Type of Engine:
Diesel

How Fast It Moves:
70 mph (112.7 kmh)

Did You Know?

Putting liquid in and taking it out has to be done carefully. Tanker cars have valves. Pipes are attached to the valves. Liquid flows in and out of the tanks.

There are two types of tanker cars. One is used to hold many different kinds of liquids. The other type is made with thicker walls and stronger steel. These cars hold more dangerous liquids such as fuel.

FUN FACT!

Workers can use safety showers to wash off any dangerous liquid.

GLOSSARY

air pressure
The weight of air molecules pressing down over an area of the earth.

boxcar
A closed railroad car with sliding doors.

cable
Very strong ropes made of steel or fiber.

commute
Travel from home to work and back again.

diesel
A type of fuel used for trains, cars, and trucks.

energy
The ability to work.

engineer
A person who designs and builds things such as buildings, bridges, and railroads.

freight
Goods shipped by train or other form of transportation such as a plane or truck.

intercity
Operating between two or more cities.

lever
A straight, strong object such as a bar used to move things.

maglev
A word that is short for "magnetic levitation."

passenger
A person riding in a vehicle such as a train.

railway
A path made of two metal rails, or tracks, that trains run on.

restored
Brought back to the way it was originally.

steam
The name for water when it is in gas form.

tram
A box-shaped vehicle that runs on rails or overhead cables.

TO LEARN MORE

More Books to Read

Gifford, Clive. *How Trains Work*. Lonely Planet Kids, 2019.

Prénat, Sophie. *Ultimate Spotlight: Trains*. Chronicle (Twirl), 2020.

Sedgman, Sam. *Epic Adventures: Explore the World in 12 Amazing Train Journeys*. Kingfisher, 2022.

Online Resources

To learn more about trains, please visit **abdobooklinks.com** or scan this QR code. These links are routinely monitored and updated to provide the most current information available.

INDEX

PHOTO CREDITS